THE SELF-PUBLISHER'S
AMAZON
PLAYBOOK

I0106463

THE AUTHOR'S MANUAL
TO CRAFTING AMAZON BOOK
LISTINGS THAT SELL

JANE TABACHNICK

Every effort has been made by the author and publishing house to ensure that the information contained in this book was correct as of press time. The conclusions and strategies presented in this book are based on the available Amazon data, credible sources, and our publishing experience. Amazon does not publicly disclose all the information or parameters influencing their search engines and algorithms. While we strive to provide accurate and helpful guidance, the ever-evolving nature of Amazon's platform may lead to variations in results. Readers are encouraged to consider this when applying the insights shared in this book.

The Self-Publisher's Amazon Playbook: The Author's Manual to Crafting Amazon Book Listings That Sell by Jane Tabachnick

Library of Congress Number: 2024921077

eBook 978-1-959009-23-8
Paperback 978-1-959009-22-1
Published in the United States by Simply Good Press

SIMPLY
GOOD PRESS
EST. 2012

PREFACE

Congratulations, author or future author.

As the founder of a book publishing consultancy, Simply Good Press, I speak to many authors. These range from published authors and soon-to-be-published authors to people just at the idea stage, staring at a blank page.

I know how much thought, energy, effort, love, blood, sweat, tears, heart, and dreams go into your book. I personally feel your pain when I hear you speak about your frustration that fewer people are reading it or that you're not getting the results you desire from it.

The good news is that it doesn't have to be that way. There are many things that you can do to help your book get discovered, seen, and read by more of your ideal audience. The best part is that these are all simple and free ways to optimize your book listing on Amazon, the giant gorilla of all bookstores.

Wherever you are on your publishing journey, this book can help you! Book listings are iterative and can be continually tweaked after publishing to build relevance and improve rankings. However, not every aspect of the book is changeable without creating a new listing with a new ISBN, which I will cover later in the book.

This book will show you exactly how to optimize your book listings, improving your visibility and book sales. It will also show you how to build out your book listing, making it look more professional and, therefore, building trust with prospects. Lastly, it will help overcome sales objections by providing more information for prospective readers to help inform their buying decisions.

I will also share the areas of optimization available to you, what tools exist to help you with the process (native Amazon tools and additional resources), and the best practices for optimizing your book listing for maximum success.

The book assumes you have a basic understanding of how to upload files to publish a book on Amazon KDP. Those basic instructions are not included in this book.

I am excited for you as you embark on this journey!

Books can change the world, one reader at a time, and I'm committed to helping you make that impact.

To your success!

With love,
Jane

TABLE OF CONTENTS

PART ONE

Getting to Know Amazon as an Author

CHAPTER ONE

Understanding Amazon

Love it or hate it, Amazon is the gorilla in book sales globally, selling twenty-eight billion dollars' worth of books worldwide every year.[1]

Amazon is more than a bookstore where you can browse titles from traditionally published, hybrid-published, and self-published authors. It is the most extensive card catalog in the world of published books, carrying books in all formats, from eBooks to paperbacks, hardcovers, and audiobooks.

Amazon generates around $28 billion worldwide from book sales every year. The company is responsible for over 50% of sales from the Big Five publishers and controls between 50% and 80% of the book distribution in the United States. Amazon sells at least 300 million print books every year.[2]

Amazon is:
- **A self-publishing platform** allowing anyone to become a published author via their Kindle Direct Publishing (KDP) platform

- **A print-on-demand publisher**
- **A search engine**
- **A discovery engine or recommendation engine** that displays a variety of results related to the product or term you are searching for, helping you discover new authors or products

As a multifaceted, multifunction platform, Amazon has a lot to offer. It can take a while for authors, especially first-time authors, to discover all that is available to them. Some authors never uncover these free tools. Reading this book will give you the knowledge to use those tools, giving you a distinct advantage and helping you sell more books!

While many of these tools are optional, I encourage you to take advantage of them. They help authors tell a better story about their book and create a more professional-looking book listing and presence on Amazon. Additionally, each tool an author uses can add incremental value to their book listing. Using these tools can give your book more opportunities to rank in different and additional sections of the Amazon site, potentially rank higher, and make a book more discoverable. All these factors can increase visibility and book sales.

One tool, A+ Content, can increase book sales by 8%[3]

This book focuses on Amazon rather than other book publishing or retail platforms for three reasons.

1. As we have detailed, Amazon is the biggest online bookseller in the world and, therefore, has the largest pool of potential buyers.

2. Amazon is a discovery engine. It is easy to browse in several different ways, from keyword searches to category browsing and the related books Amazon shows viewers based on their searches, providing multiple opportunities for authors to be discovered by new readers.

3. Thirdly, it has the most comprehensive suite of tools for book listings of any other platform, giving authors an added advantage to succeed.

[The importance of] Amazon for Authors

Amazon is a force as the most extensive online book catalog and bookseller. It is one that you should not ignore. It is the most important marketplace online for your book, and you can and should leverage it to optimize your book's success. That is why this book focuses on Amazon book listing optimization. As the leading online bookstore and discovery engine, it can help you reach the largest audience and sell more of your book. Amazon also offers the most tools for book optimization of any of the existing online booksellers. We encourage you to optimize your book's listing on every platform on which your book is available.

By listing your book in the most extensive online bookstore, you will have access to millions of potential buyers from around the globe. You will also be competing for their attention and getting your book seen by them. After that, you'll also be competing for the sale. You need to sell them and explain why your book is a better solution than your competitors' books that you are listed right next to.

For these reasons above, optimizing your book, making it easily found by your ideal audience, and looking attractive and professional to entice your prospective reader is so important. Your book's success depends on it. Writing a great book is simply not enough.

Being discoverable is less necessary for celebrity authors or authors with an existing catalog of successful books. People will search Amazon by their name or book title, pre-sold on buying their book. They will want to optimize for new topics or keywords. For new or relatively unknown authors to be visible and discoverable, it is necessary to be able to be found by prospects. Here are a few essential factors that are needed to do so:

- Good and relevant search terms
- Being in relevant and rank-able categories
- Some positive book reviews
- A professional-looking book listing
- A compelling book description

Using the best possible versions of those above and additional author marketing tools that Amazon offers gives your book the most excellent chance for success. When discussing optimizing a book, I refer to implementing these elements or improving an existing book listing based on these factors.

In a competitive marketplace, authors who use these tools and optimize their book listings have a distinct competitive advantage over those who don't. Here is an example of a book optimization we did for a client whose book on food as medicine was written for middle aged women. Simply changing their categories to relevant, but less competitive ones, we were able to achieve two #1-rankings and a #2 ranking in their categories. This created bestseller status, and a significant increase in discoverability.

Category Makeover

Product details		Product details	
Publisher : Sounds True (October 26, 2021)		Publisher : Sounds True (October 26, 2021)	
Language : English		Language : English	
Hardcover : 328 pages		Hardcover : 328 pages	
ISBN-10 : 168364719X		ISBN-10 : 168364719X	
ISBN-13 : 978-1683647195		ISBN-13 : 978-1683647195	
Item Weight : 1.67 pounds		Item Weight : 1.67 pounds	
Dimensions : 6.32 x 1.07 x 9.2 inches		Dimensions : 6.32 x 1.07 x 9.2 inches	
Best Sellers Rank: #5,314 in Books (See Top 100 in Books)		Best Sellers Rank: #6,758 in Books (See Top 100 in Books)	
#6 in Eating Disorder Self-Help		#1 in Popular Psychology & Medicine	
#55 in Other Diet Books		#1 in Antioxidants & Phytochemicals (Books)	
#262 in Personal Transformation Self-Help		#2 in Menopause (Books)	
Customer Reviews: ★★★★★ ˅ 8 ratings		Customer Reviews: ★★★★★ ˅ 12 ratings	

Category makeover we did for a client – creating bestseller status and greater visibility

Additionally, Amazon is a top authority site. According to SEMrush, it is the seventh highest-ranked website in the United States.[4] This authority ranking means that your book listing and author page on Amazon are highly likely to appear in search results for your name and topic (depending on the keywords in your title and subtitle). When someone Googles your name, your Amazon book listings can appear on page one of the search results. Associating Amazon with your name creates a powerful impression, enriched by the credibility and expert status of being a published author.

A well-optimized book will appear not just on Amazon search results but also in Google or other search engine results for a term or your topic. Being easily found in search engines can help the media, conference planners and podcast hosts find you easily when they are looking for a source or a speaker on that topic. Not only do you or your book come up in searches, but you make a great first impression with these essential new connections. It can also help prospects from entrepreneurs to large corporations find you when they're in the market for a resource, expert, consultant, or company to help them make a hire to solve a problem or need that they have.

For nonfiction authors, this can help attract opportunities.

Note: All the tools mentioned in this book can be accessed via the Amazon Kindle Direct Publishing (KDP) platform or Author Central, a related but separate free tool from Amazon.

Understanding the Amazon Buyer

Meet your Amazon buyer. They may be regular, repeat Amazon customers but have yet to buy one of your books. You are a stranger to them, so they may be skeptical of you and your book.

Unless you are a well-known expert with a visible, recognized brand, you remain just another author whom readers need to vet carefully before spending their hard-earned dollars on or wasting their time reading a book that may be of poor quality.

In business, there are warm and cold referrals. You can think of the Amazon shopper as cold traffic or a cold prospect who found you through an online search, never having heard about you previously. Imagine trying a new restaurant that you happened upon. You have never heard about it from trusted friends and colleagues and have yet to read any reviews, so you are coming to it cold. Skepticism is very high and may even deter you, a cold prospect, from trying the restaurant.

A warm referral would be someone who has heard about the restaurant via online reviews or been referred to by a friend, colleague, family member, or the media. As warm prospects, they are likelier to try the restaurant because a trusted referral source has recommended it.

The same is true for book listings. Cold traffic—the kind that Amazon shows your book to and has never heard of you before—is skeptical.

Based on their smooth buying and delivery experiences on Amazon, these prospects trust the platform. But they need to find out whether they can trust you yet. Perhaps they've bought some books on Amazon that disappointed them or were of poor quality, so they are skeptical and cautious before buying books.

Mistrust of unknown authors and brands is why your book listing is so important, especially to these cold prospects. Every aspect of it can build trust and interest or turn off even your ideal prospective buyers. And you only have a few seconds to make that positive, professional impression before the prospect moves on to check out the next book listing.

Your listing is a sales page for your book. Like any other advertisement or product listing, it must sell the prospect on why they should buy the book. Creating a sale comes down to two key things: enough information to let the prospect know if the book is for them and a professional presentation that conveys that the product is high quality and trustworthy.

How do you build trust with cold Amazon traffic so you can sell more books? Ensure your book listing is as professional, informative, and attractive as possible. A professional presentation includes good quality information, is well laid out, does not have typos or misspellings, and conveys a sense of trust in the prospects' minds.

It leads them to think that if the book listing looks this good, it will surely be of high quality.

To build trust with cold traffic, authors and publishers need the following

- Overall professional and attractive book listing with sufficient detail
- A professional-looking, attractive book cover
- A well-written, catchy, and informative book description that is well-formatted and easy to read
- A clear book promise - conveyed from the title and subtitle
- A clear idea of who the book is for
- What the reader can expect to experience, learn, or get out of reading the book
- What others have said about the book, such as editorial reviews and book reviews (social proof)

Amazon as a Search Engine

As a giant online store, a key to Amazon's success is easily finding what you are looking for amongst the over 32.8 million published titles.[5] The rapid ease of shopping on Amazon is thanks to the robust and well-designed technology platform, including the Amazon search engine.

Their technology helps shoppers easily find what they are looking for and suggests similar or related books or products they may like.

With so many books for sale, standing out and getting seen is worth paying attention to. It can distinguish between readers finding your book and being buried too far down in the search engine rankings to garner sales. Many people don't look past the first page of search results, so being ranked on page one can make a big difference.

"We have found that 20% to 30% of the shoppers will click on the book that appears at the top of the search results. That percentage quickly drops to single digits the farther you get from the top. Appearing at the top of the list increases your ability to get seen and make sales." Dave Chesson[6]

You may be familiar with website owners trying to rank on page one of Google for maximum visibility, increasing their chance of getting in front of the right customers and making sales. Amazon is very similar.

The Amazon search engine is driven by technology that rapidly considers and evaluates various factors before displaying the results. Amazon has proprietary algorithms that work behind the scenes when you search their platform.

Before diving into the specifics of optimizing your book listing, it's essential to understand the variety of ways your future readers can search for books. You can directly optimize for some of this, and Amazon's algorithms will determine the balance automatically without you having to do anything additional.

Indexing and Ranking

Two factors that drive Amazon search results are indexing and ranking. First, you need to get your book listing indexed so that it can be entered into the Amazon database, which happens after setting up your book for pre-order or publishing it on Amazon. Keyword selection is integral to your success so that your book can appear in searches for relevant keywords.

Search results can be displayed based on relevance to the search term, on the book's ranking, or both. For example, in the main search results, books will be displayed based on relevance; this is determined primarily by keywords.

When looking at the results within a category search, a book is placed in the category due to the keywords and category selection, and it will display in the order of current ranking. You can see this at work by clicking on a category in the sidebar, which will bring up the Bestsellers in that category, displayed in order of ranking by current sales.

So, both metadata and current sales results drive where and how search results show up for your books. Optimizing your book and getting more sales helps optimize your book even further, as Amazon will display your book more if it sees sales activity.

Amazon has different algorithms for organic search and advertising, which also means that the algorithms for relevancy are different for paid versus organic.

Let's look at the variety of ways that search can help display your book.

The main search feature is one that you are probably most familiar with. It is the search bar accessible from the top of the site in the Amazon header. It relies on keywords and categories to determine when you appear in search results.

Within categories. As mentioned, books will be displayed within the categories that they are placed in upon setting up your book listing, as well as some that Amazon may also determine that they fit in

Bestseller lists. These are category-specific results determined by keywords and categories and displayed based on your current sales ranking compared to the other books in the category.

Hot New Releases. Available for the first thirty days after a book is listed on Amazon, you need to have a few sales to be listed as a hot new release. Like Bestseller lists, your keywords and categories determine your inclusion in a Hot New Release category, and your sales determine your rank within the listings.

Recommendations. There are several sections that Amazon may show you to recommend related books. These results are driven by metadata such as keywords and categories, and common customer searches that include your book and one that is displayed as a recommendation. You can also try to optimize your book to appear in more of these recommendations by trying to make connections between your book and another popular one.

Book Formats. Each version of your book will be searchable within the sections for that specific format. The more formats your book is in, the more options you offer your readers, and the more real estate it gets on Amazon.

Great on Kindle is a fairly new, small section on Amazon that showcases books that meet its standards of greatness. It is based solely on book formatting and the use of X-ray content.

Other known factors that can influence your book being displayed in more places, more often, is its number of reviews. Amazon is, after all, a marketplace whose goal is to make money. The number of book reviews reflects popularity and quality and helps encourage Amazon to show your book more.

While Amazon doesn't disclose all the parameters and factors it uses to determine rankings and search results, here are the areas that we know to factor in:

- Keywords and Categories
- Title and Subtitle
- Book Description
- A+ Content
- Editorial reviews

Your book listing has a few simultaneous rankings on your listing page, as seen in the following example.

Amazon rankings for BSR and categories

As you can see, you will have up to four rankings for each version of your book—the Best Sellers Rank and the three-category rankings. Sales numbers drive these rankings at the most recent assessment.

Even though paperback and hardcover category options are the same, your book may be displayed in different categories for each version and will be ranked based on the other books within the category in the same format. So, your paperback and hardcover versions of your book can be displayed in different categories. Even if they are listed in the same categories for both formats, they will be ranked differently, as the ranking only compares them to book sales in the same format - apples to apples.

Therefore, if your book is published in eBook, paperback, hardcover, and audiobook versions, it can rank in as many as sixteen categories.

Refrain from assuming that the way you think of or would search for a book on your topic is how your prospective readers will. Instead, ask them how they would find a book on your topic, and then you can test their keywords on Amazon as outlined in this book. You can also use a keyword tool for KDP. Remember to research uniquely for each format you plan to publish your book.

The relationship between search and ranking and book sales

Your categories and keywords can help determine where your book shows up. Your book sales determine your position within each category or section.

For example, my book Zoom Meetings is in the *Web Services* category. The entire category string is:

‹ Books ‹ Computers & Technology ‹ Web Development & Design ‹ **Web Services**

Now that my category is settled, Amazon search technology compares the book sales (over a specific, undisclosed time frame) to those of the other books in the category, and my book's ranking within the category is determined. That is how my book shows up as 505 within Web Services for the paperback version of my book. These rankings are updated multiple times throughout the day.

The categories are fairly set, though Amazon may occasionally adjust which ones you show up in. Your rankings, however, are continually changing based on sales—yours and that of your competitor's books. Of course, if you are number one in the category, or it is not a very active category, your rankings may not change very often.

While your book will often be listed in the categories you select and input into your KDP dashboard, you may see it appear in other categories. This is because Amazon's search technology determines if another category is a fit for your book. Remember, Amazon is focused on delivering a great customer experience, which includes making it easy to get great results based on your search terms. Having your book show up in relevant searches is a part of that.

CHAPTER TWO

Book Optimization

What exactly is optimizing a book [listing]?

Many aspects of your book—both visible and invisible—contribute to its discoverability by potential readers. Optimization helps it show up for the correct search terms or keywords, which display your book in searches and relevant categories where your ideal reader is looking for a book on your topic. It accomplishes this by harnessing the available aspects covered in this book. The more optimization you do, the more you increase your book's opportunities to be shown to your potential readers.

Behind the scenes, you have book metadata. Ingram Spark defines it like this: "Simply put, your book metadata is data that describes your book—including title, subtitle, price, publication date, ISBN, and any other relevant information readers use to find your book. Readers depend on good metadata to find their next read."[7]

There is also information that goes into your book listing on KDP that isn't seen by customers but helps tell their search engine how to index your book. One example is the seven keywords you can add to your book listing. These inform Amazon search engines where to show your book but aren't displayed on your book listing for shoppers to see.

Then, there are all the client-facing elements that will create an impression of the author and the book. These include your book cover, title, description, format, book categories, and more.

These elements, both behind the scenes and front and center, can be utilized to your maximum advantage. The process of enhancing them makes up what we call book optimization.

Many authors, especially first-time authors, create their book listings based on what they think the listing should be. They will think about and brainstorm keywords and select the ones they feel are most relevant. While authors hopefully have done their homework and know as much as possible about their ideal reader avatar, this method doesn't factor in all the available data collected by Amazon, data that can show you exactly what terms or keywords prospects use to search for a book on your topic, as well as the search volume and level of competition surrounding a specific term.

Optimizing a book involves:
- Utilizing available elements.
- Researching the best options.
- Leveraging available data.
- Implementing these strategies in your book listing to maximize its chances of success.

Your book competes with all the other books on your topic for readers' attention and with the savvy authors who employ optimization strategically, giving them a decided advantage.

Who is optimization for?

Every author and publisher can benefit from book optimization. Ignoring it is akin to leaving money on the table.

The great news about optimizing your book listing is that it can be done at any time along your publishing journey—from when you first list your book for presale to when you publish it to optimizing and improving your listing after your book is published.

Think of optimizing as an iterative process. You can change it at any time, now or in the future. This means you can optimize your book in stages, one element at a time. You can edit, monitor, and tweak your listing to improve it.

Editing Your Book Listing – A Few Restrictions

It's important to note that not all changes to your listing can be made as needed. Here are a few conditions to be aware of:

- Preorders may only be edited once, and your publishing date must be more than five days away.
- Some aspects of a book, such as the title or subtitle, can't be changed without having to issue a new ISBN. This should not be done lightly, as doing so will cause you to lose any book reviews you have already received.

How to get started doing your optimization

It starts with a great book that has been professionally edited and well formatted, with an attractive and professional-quality cover design. Professional doesn't have to mean having a skilled professional create elements of your book, though that is often the best-case scenario. Some software programs help you edit or format your book for publishing on Amazon, and the results can vary depending on the skill or taste level of the user. These tools can deliver professional results, but without professional training or experience, a user may not know that their generated outcome is not at the professional level. Yet, they unknowingly use them anyway, rendering their book less than professional quality.

I hate to see a good book go unsold and unread because the author didn't execute it professionally. When done poorly, these aspects can kill sales. It is easy to find one, or two-star Amazon reviews that mention these facts.

By optimizing your book listing, you have multiple opportunities to inform your prospective readers about the book, create a sense of trust, and build on that trust with each element of the listing, helping move a prospect to decide to buy your book.

The next step in book optimization is understanding the available book metadata options and all the book listing options Amazon offers. Some of the metadata functions behind the scenes help your book show up in relevant searches – it is used to inform Amazon so it can help readers find your book. Other metadata are displayed publicly on your book listing page for prospects to read. We'll cover both types in this book, so you're in the right place!

Some details or sections are required, and some are optional, as we'll cover in the book. Even if metadata or a section is mandatory, such as a book description, you can still optimize it for your benefit. To learn more about metadata, read this article from Fordham Press: https://bit.ly/selfpubbook1

If you haven't already, now would be a good time to set up your Author Central account. We'll cover how to optimize it fully in a later chapter.

What tools do you need to optimize your book listing?

Using special tools to optimize is unnecessary, but it can speed up the process and provide more data.

To get started with optimization, you can use the Amazon platform for research. You can also use tools like Publisher Rocket or KDSpy. I have included a resource list at the end of the book.

Amazon keyword search

Starting with the Amazon search bar up top, when you start to type into it, the 'autosuggest' feature immediately starts to populate the top and available options. These results give you the terms buyers use to search for the topic.

If you then click on a specific term, Amazon shows you how many searches there are for that term, as in the example below:

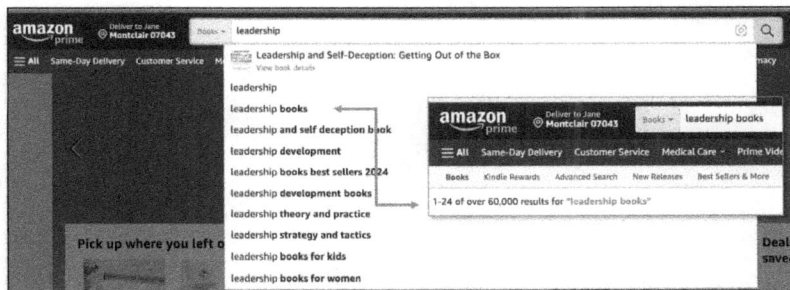

Amazon search results — the number of searches for a term or keyword

By trying a few terms, we can compare and see which gets the most searches. Often, a more popular term is also more competitive, so you'll want to weigh all available information when doing your research before finalizing your input.

You can also use competitive analysis to provide insights into keywords and categories.

While we can't determine what keywords a book has input when it shows up in results for a specific keyword, it has either been optimized for that term in at least one section or placed there by Amazon after the algorithm determined it should show up in those results.

We can also use Amazon to see what categories a similar competitor has used to give us category suggestions. You are allowed to select three categories for your book. Amazon may place it in those categories as well as additional categories.

CHAPTER THREE

Setting up your hub, Author Central

One of Amazon's most recognized tools for authors is the Author Central feature. It's part marketing tool and part sales dashboard. It allows authors to create a custom landing page for their books. The Author Central page is different from the book listing page on Amazon.com.

Author Central currently exists in six Amazon marketplaces: the United States, the United Kingdom, Germany, France, Japan, and Brazil.

According to Amazon: "Amazon Author Central lets you create your Author Page to share the most up-to-date information about yourself and your books with millions of readers. It helps readers find your books easily and in one place."[8]

Unlike your Amazon book listing page, which has designated sections and content automatically populated by the platform, the main Author Central page—the Author Bio—comprises content you input.

Author Central is a separate but connected Amazon site; you must sign up for your account. There are three elements of Author Central:

1. Your author profile (content)
2. Your book catalog
3. Sales dashboard

Amazon allows you to post content under the 'author profile,' which is the central part of your book landing page. On the U.S. version of Author Central, you can only post an author photo along with your text; in all the Author Central marketplaces, you can also post additional pictures and videos.

An author bio is a great way to introduce your readers to who you are, your background, and how they can learn more about you. This information is valuable as readers want to get to know the writer of a book and learn more about them. By introducing them to the writer, your author bio helps provide a sense of know, like, and trust. It can also provide insight into the author's motivation to write a book or series.

Optimizing your Profile for More Sales

While your author profile content doesn't get indexed, it is searchable on Amazon and benefits authors in a few additional ways. Once your author profile is created and you have connected your books, your profile is accessible from your book listing page by a hyperlink. This connection makes it easy for prospective readers visiting your book listing page on

Amazon.com by clicking on your name and be taken over to your author profile.

Your author profile is indexed by search engines such as Google, Bing, and Duck Duck Go, and it will show among the first five results in any search engine. Anyone checking you out via an online search will instantly see that you are a published author, which is a great credibility booster,

Google search result for Jane Tabachnick – the Amazon listing shows up as the 2nd result

Google search example – the Amazon listing shows up at the top of the page in this case as the second result.

Another feature of Author Central is creating your book catalog and showcasing all your published books in one place. When readers discover you, they can easily see all the books you have authored, which can lead to multiple purchases.

You need to add books to your listing to create your book catalog. Amazon asks you to 'claim' your book to be added to your profile. You need to do this individually for each version of the book.

Optimizing your author profile for more sales includes a well-rounded biography. As mentioned, your reader wants to get to know you and gain insights into your background and what makes you a credible expert or author. Sharing your philosophy and motivations can help build connections and trust. Prospects like to connect on a human level, which can be achieved by including your author's photo. Outside of the U.S. marketplace, authors can post additional pictures and videos. A bonus feature of Author Central is the ability to add your biography in multiple languages. This can be an asset to interested readers in other markets who want to learn more about you. Even if your book is only available in English, you may reach and convert more prospective readers when you include a bio in the primary language of their marketplace.

To help boost your connection with your readers and build out your author platform, you'll want to include links to where they can follow you on social media and your website address. Unfortunately, Author Central doesn't allow live hyperlinks, so visitors can't click through to your website or social media accounts, but it is still valuable to list them. Please take advantage of your profile to create further engagement with your audience by letting them know you are interested and available for speaking gigs and podcast guest interviews.

The author profile doesn't allow the use of HTML, so you are constrained to simple text without the ability to add headings, bold, italics, etc.

The Sales Dashboard

Author Central offers a sales dashboard with more detailed information than what is available in the KDP backend. This dashboard includes:

- ☐ Check Amazon Best Sellers Rank
- ☐ Check Customer Reviews

☐ Check BookScan* sales information (U.S. feature only)

☐ Check the number of Amazon followers

*BookScan is an independent service aggregating book sales across booksellers, not just Amazon.

While you can find the Best Seller's Rank and Customer Reviews on your book listing page, it's nice to see them in one easy view, along with the additional information included with the BookScan data and followers count.

The other optimization feature available through Author Central is the ability to add Editorial Reviews to your book listing page (U.S. Marketplace only). We discuss this feature in more detail in Chapter 9.

As a hub, Author Central benefits you, your readers, and your prospects by having author information in one convenient place accessible with one click via your book listing on Amazon.com. As with other optimization aspects, your author hub could be the additional information that helps sway prospective readers to buy your book.

PART TWO

Tools and Tactics to Optimize Your Book Listing

CHAPTER FOUR

Setting up Strong Categories and Keywords

Categories and Keywords are the most noteworthy of the Amazon optimization tools. Their importance is due to the fact that most people start their search in the main search bar at the top of the Amazon website. The results returned from searches are driven by algorithms whose fuel is derived from categories and keywords. An author's ability to appear in search results on Amazon is critical to being visible, discoverable, and reaching your ideal readers.

Categories and keywords can be changed as often as you like. However, I don't recommend changing them daily. You'll want to give your selections a chance and see where your book lands in the various categories and how well they rank over time before making changes. Amazon doesn't disclose how often they update their book rankings; we have seen updates as frequently as multiple times in one day. Your book's ranking is not static; it depends on how many volumes you sell compared to the other books in the category.

Keywords

There are two types of keywords to consider. The ones you think your customer will use to find your book or topic. The other set is based on how Amazon customers search for your topic. It may surprise you that the primary keywords or terms you think are the best are not the ones most used on Amazon. Using the data available from Amazon can be crucial to increasing your book sales.

Two ways to access Amazon keyword and category data are through the Amazon platform or third-party tools. Book research tools such as KDP Rocket or KDP Spy offer a quick and thorough way to see keyword or category popularity data. They also show competitive sales numbers, rankings, and more.

You can also use the Amazon platform to check keyword popularity, though it's more time-consuming. Start by using the autosuggest feature that appears below the main search bar. When you input a term or keyword, Amazon populates a drop-down menu below, which shows the number of searches for a specific term.

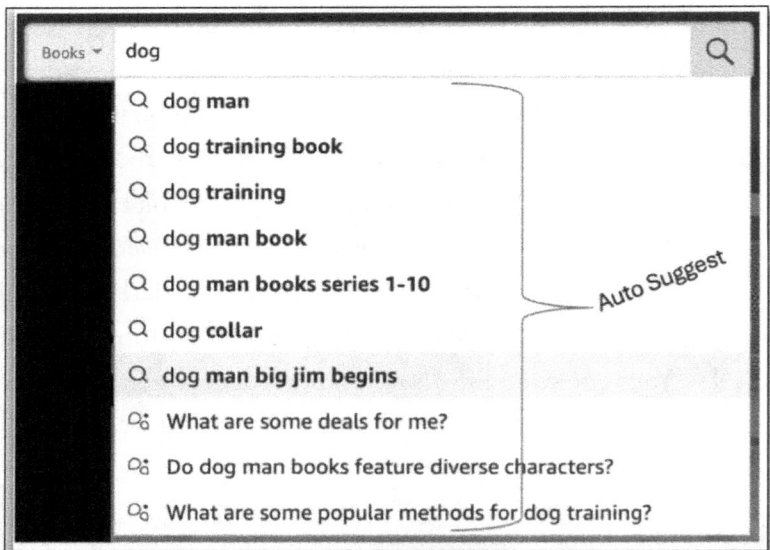

Autosuggest example

Remember that more competitive terms often mean more competition, so you must balance the number of searches made on Amazon with the number of products in a category and how many reviews a product has garnered. This research is quickly done via the paid tools but may require guesswork if you rely on autofill and your impressions of the category listings alone.

Amazon's number one book sells the most copies on the platform.

Product details

Publisher : Avery; First Edition (October 16, 2018)

Language : English

Hardcover : 320 pages

ISBN-10 : 0735211299

ISBN-13 : 978-0735211292

Item Weight : 1.13 pounds

Dimensions : 6.28 x 1.07 x 9.27 inches

UNSPSC-Code : 55101500 (Printed publications) Report an incorrect code

Best Sellers Rank: #24 in Books (See Top 100 in Books)

   #1 in Personal Transformation Self-Help

   #2 in Parenting (Books)   **Categories**

   #3 in Popular Social Psychology & Interactions

Customer Reviews: 4.8 ★★★★★ ∨   133,527 ratings

Where to find BSR and categories

An individual book has two sets of rankings—the overall BSR in the Amazon store and its category rankings.

Your BSR compares your book's sales to all books on the Amazon store in the same format (eBooks to eBooks) and ranks you in order of how many books were sold during the tracking period (it could be an hour or a day). This ongoing data comparison is why the BSR fluctuates so often.

Your category rankings—up to three categories—are based on how well your book is selling compared to the other books in the category in the same format.

For each version of your book, you have four rankings - the BSR rank in all of Amazon, i.e., #14 BSR in Kindle Store for your eBook, and the three category rankings, each of which have their rankings against the other eBooks listed in their respective category. There will be another set of 4 rankings for each version - for the paperback, hardcover, and audiobook.

Understanding Categories

Categories are public facing. You are allowed three category selections per format. While your book will primarily be shown in these three categories, Amazon may also place your book in different or additional categories. Amazon algorithms dynamically drive this placement, which you can't completely control.

Before selecting categories, it is helpful to understand how Amazon has created them. It helps to think of categories like a tree with branches. The main topics are the big branches, with many smaller branches attached. Subcategories are the smaller branches; they sit under the main categories. These subcategories get more specific and targeted at each level you go down from the main category.

A significant category is Health, Fitness and Dieting. It is incredibly competitive and general as the leading, broad topic category. The branches that shoot off from it are specific, related categories, some of which have their associated subcategories. You can get a sense of them in this category string, where Exercise & Fitness is a more specific topic under its parent (Health, Fitness & Dieting), and Ab Workouts is an even more specific category within Exercise & Fitness.

Here is the category string:
‹ Books ‹ Health, Fitness & Dieting ‹ Exercise & Fitness ‹ Ab Workouts

While there is no way to see all the categories and subcategories in one place, Amazon doesn't give you a complete list of categories to select from in the KDP dashboard, and there is no published list of all the ones in existence. You can see many of them in a sidebar listing on Amazon or using a keyword tool.

How to Find Categories

1. **Research competitors**. Examining recently published books on your topic and identifying their categories is an excellent way to get ideas for potential book categories.

   But do this with care—just because a competitor's book ranks in a category doesn't mean it's the best for your book. You'll want to check how competitive the category is before deciding if it's a good fit.
2. **Search specific terms**. Search for a term you believe people will use to find your book and see what books come up. Open the listings to examine a few of the top titles. List their categories and determine if they fit your book listing.

3. **The Sidebar on Amazon to explore subcategories.** Go into the Kindle store or books tab in the top navigation bar and enter a search term. The results will include a left sidebar with a list of all the categories for the particular Amazon format you selected. When you click on the main categories, the subcategories will be revealed, or sub-subcategories if they exist. Not all categories have subcategories or third-level categories, so I encourage you to click and expand the listings to find all the branches of the trees and see all available options.

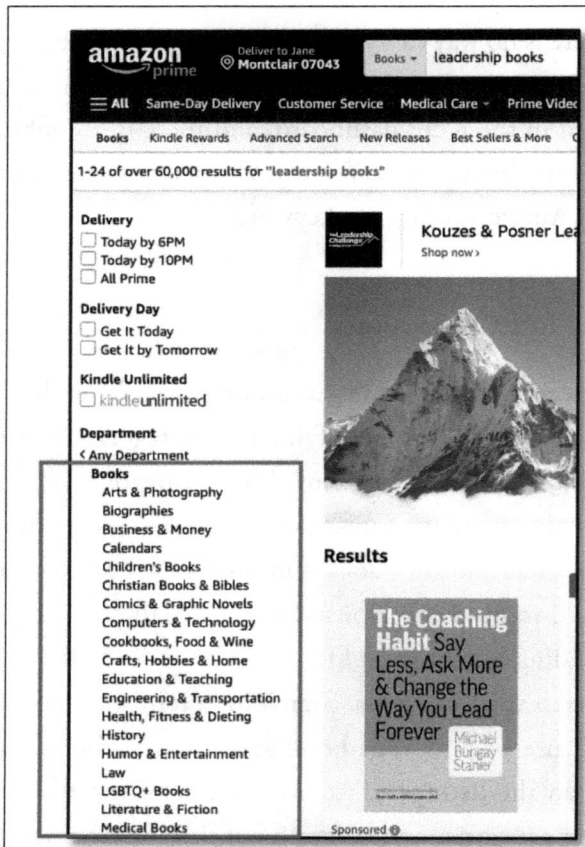

Categories location in Amazon sidebar

4. **Use KDP**. When you select your categories in the KDP dashboard, you can see the options available, but it is not set up intuitively nor is it easy to use. Sometimes, you must dig to find a category you have identified via the previous three methods. I recommend doing your homework via the first three methods and only using option four to input categories rather than using it as a research method.

Create a list of at least ten potential categories to choose from. Then, you'll want to evaluate them for relevance and rankability.

Relevance is important. I sometimes see romance novels listed in low-competition business categories. Listing in a category that isn't relevant isn't a good strategy, nor is it optimizing your book for your ideal readers. While it may give you a great low ranking in the category, no one is looking for a romance novel in business leadership, so it won't help display your book to those interested. A book listing like this suggests the author is trying to game the system, which could hurt the trust of the reader audience.

Another method for doing category research is to look at competitor book listings. In the product details section of the book listing, you can see the categories it is listed in, just under its bestseller rank. You will see up to three categories the book is currently listed in; displayed is the end of the string or the most specific category the book is listed in. You will only see part of the category string, which you need to know. To view the string, just click on a category in the listing, and it will open the sidebar panel to show you all the branches in the string. Copy them down for future use, so you have them when you are ready to input your book's categories. The category string for the example below, *Workplace Culture*, is:

Books > Business & Money >Business Culture > **Workplace Culture**

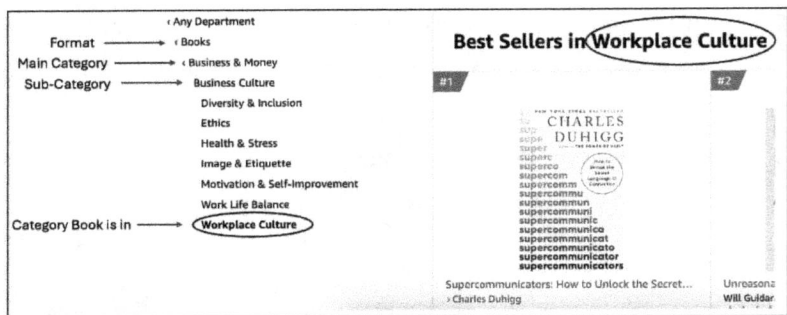

Amazon sidebar expanded to display categories and subcategories

It's also worth noting that the categories for print books differ from the available categories for eBooks or audiobooks, so it is essential to research each format separately to arrive at your book's best and most available options.

Categories, like your book's overall ranking, can change. Your book may move in and out of categories—the three you select and other category placements determined by Amazon. This movement is based on Amazon's algorithms and will happen automatically and without notice. For the most part, your book will display in the categories you select if they are relevant to your title and metadata.

What makes a category rankable?

Whether a book is traditionally published or self-published doesn't indicate that the author has done an excellent job listing it, so only copy their categories after thoroughly researching them to ensure they are the best ones for your listing.

Categories are not the same for eBooks, print books, or audio-books. While many main categories are available, the subcategories differ for your various book formats. For example, you may have to select a different subcategory for your eBook because the one you choose for your print book is not available for eBooks. Therefore, to optimize your book listing correctly, you will want to do unique keyword research for each book format to ensure you place it in the optimal categories.

This often comes as a surprise to authors, but you may not find an exact match category for your topic. Some categories that you would think are common or popular enough to warrant a dedicated category such as 'emotional intelligence' do not have one. Or they exist in one format such as eBook, but not in print.

In this case, you will want to find the most relevant categories for your book, even if they are not an exact match from format to format.

Strike a balance between relevant categories and rankable ones. For example, the best category for your book is one where the top three books are bestselling books (N.Y. Times or WSJ bestselling books), with over one hundred reviews each. In that case, there is a good chance the category is extremely competitive, and you won't be able to be easily discovered in that category or show up in the top one hundred on page one.

This is not to suggest that being number one in a category is the only acceptable measure of success for an author. It is the metric we use to start evaluating a category for rankability. We also look at the number of reviews. A book that ranks well in a category but has a low number of reviews can signal that the category is not highly competitive because the more sales a book has, the more reviews it typically gathers over time.

For example, a top, broad category is *Health, Fitness & Dieting*. At the date of this printing, the number one book in Health, Fitness & Dieting is the new memoir by Lisa-Marie Presley, an internationally known celebrity.

To reach the number one book in this category in Kindle format, you need to sell 1909 books a day. Unless you are a celebrity or have a book that has caught on like wildfire, this is an unattainable, unrankable category. A subcategory of *Health, Fitness & Dieting* is *Ab Workouts*, a rankable category – it takes 11 books sold in one day to reach number one.

Rankability Review					
Category (Main)	Book Title	Rank in Category	(Overall) BSR in Kindle Store	# of Reviews	# of books sold per day
Health, Fitness & Dieting	From Here to the Great Unknown: A Memoir By Lisa-Marie Presley	1	40	989	1909
Health, Fitness & Dieting	Thanks a Thousand: A Gratitude Journey (TED) A. J. Jacobs	50	4,792	522	38
We looked at a sub-subcategory of Health, Fitness & Dieting					
Ab Workout	The Year One Challenge for Men by Michael Matthews	1	25,057	1852	11
Ab Workout	The 6 Week Upper Body Fix by Doug Bennet	50	556,375	36	Less than a book a day

Rankability Comparison

Category and keyword research can be learned, though it may take a while to master it. Selecting the right categories and keywords requires discipline and avoiding letting emotions take over.

While you may want to rank in a specific category, if it is highly competitive, consider a less competitive subcategory. Unless you are a celebrity or have a huge author platform and online following, it will be hard to compete in a highly competitive category over the long term, resulting in your book not getting seen very much by your ideal reader.

Category and keyword research can be easily and affordably outsourced. You'll want to hire a consultant who uses a tool or set of tools to conduct research. Getting this intel can be some of the best money you spend on your book. It can also be very affordable and efficient. Rather than buy a research tool or software, you can put the money into hiring a consultant and save yourself the time it would take to try and learn how to use the tools.

CHAPTER FIVE

Creating Your Title and Subtitle

The title of your book is more than simply a name. It can identify the work, give it context, convey a minimal summary of its contents, and pique a potential reader's curiosity, thereby impacting buying decisions.

A title can do the following for your book:

- Attract
- Intrigue
- Create curiosity
- Inform
- Describe
- Help SEO through keywords and terms
- Sell

Amazon uses the title and subtitle to index your book so that it can appear in relevant searches. Therefore, optimizing your title and subtitle for better search results can increase your discoverability greatly, thereby increasing sales opportunities.

Readers want to know what the book is about and what type of book it is. Is it a collection of stories, a way to learn about a subject or a more instructional how-to guide? They want to understand what they can expect to learn or experience from reading the book. To avoid disappointing readers ' expectations, the promise of your book needs to be clear in your title (and subtitle if one is used). Doing so can result in negative reviews and book returns.

Subtitles

An author can decide to use only a title for their book, or they can also use a title paired with a subtitle. While subtitles are optional, they can describe the book and deliver information the title may not convey. Both elements are extremely important aspects of your book. They help prospects decide if the book is for them and influence buying decisions.

Your title and subtitle combined must be fewer than 200 characters on Amazon, so you want to use them wisely and maximize their role in your book's success.

Your book's title and subtitle are important positioning elements to attract your ideal reader. They can call in your reader, share the promise of your book, let the prospect know who the book is for, and even call out the book's style (more about this in a moment). They also offer another opportunity to optimize your book listing for keywords and terms. Your title and subtitle are searchable and play a vital role in the main search results.

The clearer your title is about the book, the better the chances it will help sell it to your ideal readers.Specificity in your title is a good strategy. While vague or catchy names may sound sexy, they don't work for most nonfiction books except under the following two conditions:

You are famous or have a descriptive subtitle explaining the book's promise.

For example, the bestseller Spare has a catchy title that works well for Prince Harry, who is famous but wouldn't work well for anyone else. In this case, the title refers to his position in line with the throne of England and works because his name is attached to the book. The title used by anyone else is too vague to know what the book was about.

Another example is the book KNOWN by Mark Schaefer, which works well because a strong subtitle supports it. Known is an intriguing title, but on its own, it needs to offer more information to determine exactly what the book promises. Is it a memoir of a celebrity? Is it about telepathy or clairvoyance? You get the idea.

KNOWN as a title is a bit vague on its own and would leave prospective readers unsure of what the book is about or whether it is for them. Schaefer has used a subtitle to ensure the book resonates with its intended audience and leaves no question about what it is about. Here is the full title and subtitle:

KNOWN: The Handbook for Building and Unleashing Your Personal Brand in the Digital Age.

The subtitle conveys the following information
- **What** type of book it is: a handbook

- **Who** it is for: anyone interested in building a personal brand
- **Where:** in the digital age [meaning in an online and social media world]

Many authors pick a title based on what they think will attract their ideal readers or on words that sound good to them. This selection method can result in a good or great-sounding title. However, in a very competitive environment like the Amazon marketplace, you need to do some keyword research before finalizing a title to avoid ending up with a title that won't help you get discovered.

Granted, creating your title doesn't require keyword research, but as the title is one of the most critical aspects of your book for attracting clients, it's strongly recommended. Your prospects will judge and evaluate your book based on the title, cover, and general look of the listing.

As one of the critical factors that Amazon uses to rank and display your book on their site, authors who optimize their titles have a distinct advantage over those who don't, assuming we compare quality books.

Using Keywords to Optimize Your Title

John wants to write a book on how to do a book launch. He is considering the title: How to Run a Successful Book Launch. It's a clear title that lets you know the book's promise of what you will learn. Let's see if this is the best title using available data.

Keyword Research			
Keyword	**Competitors**	**Monthly Earnings (Average)**	**Monthly Searches**
Book Launch	>1000	$367	<100
We looked at a few alternative terms:			
Book Marketing	>1000	$3974	785
Book Promotion	>1000	$295	<100

Keyword comparison - example of data provided by a research tool

As you can see from the three terms we analyzed, Book Marketing gets seven times the monthly searches on Amazon and makes over ten times the sales of the other terms. Granted, it is also a more competitive, more popular search term.

Use this keyword knowledge to your advantage when selecting your title and subtitle

Now that you have data to help inform your book name, you can use the terms in either your title or subtitle to help give it a better chance of being ranked for one of these or both terms so that your ideal prospect will discover it when they search for a book on your topic.

Since John's book is about book launches, I recommend using book launch and book marketing in his title and subtitling so that it can appear in searches for both terms. As an example, his title could be:

> Book Marketing Success Using a Repeat Book Launch Strategy
> Or
> The Author's Book Marketing Guide
> How to Run a Successful Book Launch Campaign (subtitle)

Your title and subtitle can, therefore, convey key information about your book to a prospective reader or searcher on Amazon. They can also be optimized to convey the same meaning and attract your ideal reader while using choice keywords and terms to help your book get discovered more.

Keep your title sounding natural. The excessive use of key terms can make the title sound stilted and result in an adverse reaction, as readers will easily notice this approach. Amazon will occasionally push back and ask you to change a title that is clearly stuffed.

If your book hasn't been published yet and it's time to brainstorm its title and subtitle, here is how to do it.

Action Steps

- Draft a title and subtitle. Do not yet become wedded to it. Draft a few versions of it.
- Outline who it is for
- Outline the book's promise (what will they get out of it ?)
- Decide the style of the book (guide, handbook, memoir)
- What stage of knowledge is the ideal reader at? (For example, my Zoom book is for beginners)

Note: If your book has already been published, then changing the title is not something to do without careful consideration. Any change in your title or subtitle will require an entirely new book listing. The revised listing would require obtaining a new ISBN and cover design and updating your book listing. Additionally, any book reviews or ranking for your current listing will not transfer to the new book, so you will lose them.

CHAPTER SIX

All About A+ Content

Amazon offers authors a section for bonus content called A+ (A Plus) Content. Formerly known as Enhanced Brand Content (EBC), it is a free tool available via the KDP publishing platform that allows authors to add graphics to their book listing to make it visually engaging and provide additional information to help inform prospective buyers.

With A+ Content, sellers can add branding and brand stories, detailed product shots, additional information, and more about the author and the book. This extra content goes beyond what is available in the basic book listing and is used well. A+ Content can increase book sales.

Basic A+ Content can increase sales by up to 8%—and well-implemented Premium A+ Content can increase sales by up to 20%.[9]

The standard Amazon Book listing only allows authors to use text of up to two thousand characters, with no images or graphics other than the book cover. With A+ Content, authors can showcase the product's distinguishing features, benefits, rave reviews, and brand story in a compelling way.

A+ Content can optimize your book listing in two important ways, which I'll cover in-depth in this chapter:

- SEO Value
- Improve your book listing by providing valuable additional information to help buyers make decisions and build trust. Quality information and attractive, professional-looking graphics help this section compete with traditionally published books and give you the ability to look like you have a big publishing team behind you, which can inspire buyer confidence.

A + Content appears near the middle of a book listing under "From the Publisher."

From Amazon:

Add A+ Content to your detail page to make your book stand out, connect readers with your books, and share more about your author's story. When you add A+ Content to your detail page, it's located under the From the Publisher section. While the location varies, most readers must scroll to view the content.

You can create A+ Content from the KDP Marketing page. You will go to the A+ Content Manager to lay out and submit your content. When you create A+ Content, you can choose between modules to create a layout. After you've added modules to your layout, you can re-order and remove modules, add images, and add text.

The look and material of A+ Content sections can vary significantly from book to book, even within the same genre. Authors have total control over the layout design, as well as the content. But when used wisely, it will optimize your book listing and increase sales conversions.

A+ content is made up of images, though it can display text. It offers authors a way to enhance their book listing by telling a visual story or stories. A relevant picture can convey any idea more effectively than text or voice alone.

Since many prospects will quickly scan your book listing, the A+ Content offers a way to reach them more quickly, as visual information is processed more rapidly than text. "The human brain processes images 60,000 times faster than text, and 90 percent of information transmitted to the brain is visual."[10]

The graphical nature of the A + content section creates a scroll stop, as it often looks very different from the rest of the book listing. This effect adds intrigue and curiosity. It also provides an opportunity to enhance the information contained in your book listing and description. This provides prospects with more information to help them make a buying decision.

A+ Content can use up to seven modules of content. These can be configured in several ways and with various content, so the possibilities are endless. Amazon offers several templates featuring graphic boxes of different sizes for you to select from. Some of these graphic templates have editable text areas built into them. You can also make up your images and upload them if they fit the pixel size specified by Amazon.

Example of A+ Content

To create the best A+ Content, consider the following:

Let's face it. A prospect who discovers your book on Amazon has yet to learn from you or trust you. They may trust Amazon, but they need to figure out you or the quality of your book. They are cold traffic landing on your book listing.

In his book Endless Referrals, one of my favorite authors, Bob Burg, coined the phrase, Know Like Trust. He said: "All things being equal, people will do business with, and refer business to, those people they know, like, and trust."[11]

Therefore, providing prospects with as much information, features, benefits, and even social proof as possible increases your trustworthiness in their eyes, giving them the confidence to take a chance and buy your book.

What to include in your A+ Content to increase trust:

- Professional graphics
- No typos or grammatical errors
- Social proof such as testimonials, book endorsements, media mentions
- An author photo—people want to get to know you
- Additional views of the book, such as a stack of books
- Interior views and features
- Instructions on how to use the book
- Who the book is for
- What you will learn or experience from the book

How to use A+Content:

Focus on your reader. What questions might they have about your book? What unique content do you have that they would need to learn about by reading the book description? Even a nonfiction, self-help book can have non-text-based content that would increase the prospects' interest in and perception of the book's value. This could be in the form of worksheets, charts and tables, breakout boxes, or end-of-chapter action steps. Your A+ content section is an ideal place to showcase it.

Share your book's secret sauce. What is unique about your book that the reader needs to know? Show it as much as you can using visuals and tell the reader about it using the text.

Provide more information about the book. Perhaps answer a few frequently asked questions.

Showcase additional features of the book. These can include added-value sections of the book such as worksheets, charts, or indexes.

Use social proof to boost trust and credibility. People could be mistrusting about what you say about your book, but they do trust book endorsements, media quotes and book reviews, even if they don't know the endorser personally. Including some of these in your A+ Content is a great way to reinforce the know, like, and trust experience.

Optimization and A+ Content

Besides visually enhancing your book listing, A+ Content helps turn prospects into buyers by providing additional product information. It is also searchable and, therefore, can help boost your discoverability on Amazon.

While images aren't searchable, Amazon allows you to add Alt Text or keywords to each image. If you have more than one image, consider using different keywords in each image to maximize the variety of terms that will be searchable. The Alt Text is intended to help screen reader applications, so try to have them describe the image while incorporating your keywords.

A caution from Amazon: "Submitting image alt-text (previously known as image keywords) that does not describe the image and that would not be useful for a customer using a screen reader application can result in content rejection."

Example of A+ content

The Perfect Story is an excellent example of using A+ content to help inform buying decisions. The top banner shares the book's promise. The middle banner provides social proof via the book endorsements, which are especially powerful due to the recognizable names. The third banner expands on the content by letting us know who the book is for and the various occasions and situations that the Perfect Story can help with.

Example of A+ content

Additionally, Amazon offers a free tool to help your book listing stand out and provide prospective readers with more information to help them decide if they want to buy the book. Using A+ Content will help your book look professional, showcase book additional book features, and help prospects reach buying decisions.

A+ content can increase your book sales in a few ways:

- **Use of Alt Tags**–additional SEO terms that can help increase your book's discoverability and visibility on Amazon.
- **Enhanced information**–providing additional information can help inform prospects and sell them further on your book
- **Professional presentation**–your listing looks professional, which increases prospect trust, helping them feel confident buying a book from an unknown author

Amazon has strict guidelines around A+ Content, so reviewing them before creating your content is a good idea. You can review those guidelines in the book's resource section.

CHAPTER SEVEN

Book Descriptions and Formatting

Book Descriptions

The book description is a synopsis found on your book listing page. Like your title and subtitle, your book description has multiple roles to play in your book's success. If you think of your title like the window display, it is designed to inform and entice your prospect into your bookstore. Inside, they are intrigued enough by your title to want to find out more; now, your book description's job is to deepen the intrigue and compel them to action.

A strong book description has three main sections:
- the headline
- the body
- the call to action

Like your book's title, the description headline needs to capture attention and the desire to learn more about the book. It must draw the prospect in to continue learning more and read the full description. This can be done in a few ways, including intrigue, a bold statement, humor, or relatability.

Optimization opportunities for your book description include SEO keywords and terms, identifying audiences, and highlighting formats such as a how-to guide or step-by-step. Length is a factor in a successful book description, as you maximize the text that can be included in SEO. Amazon allows you 4000 characters for the description.

The other optimization option, from a prospect's point of view, is formatting. For your book listing to look professional, formatting the description will make it easier to read while enhancing buyer confidence.

Formatting—Hello to white space and design elements

An excellent book description is about more than just the words you write. It needs to be easy to read and attractive to the eye.

This is where formatting comes in. Formatting is how text is laid out on a page. It can include bold, italics, different-size fonts, bullets or numbered lists, and white space.

Amazon allows you to control your book description formatting. The KDP platform uses modified HTML, the software language behind simple formatting on many websites.

As mentioned earlier in the book, people scan pages quickly. So, it's helpful to have key information stand out to grab their attention and get them to stop scrolling and read your book description. Key information can be made to stand out with bolded text or some other formatting feature.

Here is an example of formatting using HTML in the book description:

Example of HTML formatted book description

White space is an underutilized aspect of formatting. Because people tend to scan text, shorter paragraphs with white space in between work better and are much easier to read than big, long paragraphs.

Here is an example of a book description that wasn't well formatted and what it looks like with good, attractive formatting.

Book description makeover we did - before and after HTML formatting

Based on the original formatting, it is possible that cold traffic to this book listing would be concerned about purchasing the book based on the look of the description. They could also assume that the book itself would need better formatting and be hard to read, turning off prospective buyers and losing sales.

CHAPTER EIGHT

Maximizing Book Reviews

Book reviews play an important role in the success of your book for three main reasons.

Book reviews help sell books. They are key to garnering book sales for three main reasons: social proof, conveying additional information (unbiased, third-party feedback), and Amazon SEO.

Books without reviews or with just a few reviews (under ten) are like great but empty restaurants. People are skeptical of a book with few reviews, just as they hesitate to go into an empty restaurant.

Fast food chain Orange Julius was acutely aware of the 'empty restaurant problem' and its significant impact on their bottom line. To combat this, they promoted a free drink to anyone who came into their restaurant when it was completely empty. Why? They knew that people were naturally skeptical of going into an empty restaurant. Diners will assume there is something wrong with it. If there is at least one person in the restaurant, then there is social proof in the form of an existing, live customer, increasing buyer confidence. Orange Julius incentivized diners to come in when the restaurant was empty to minimize having an empty restaurant and risking turning away skeptical diners. Their offer of a free drink to anyone who came in when the restaurant had no customers was enough to overcome "empty restaurant reluctance."

The same is true for your book listing. No reviews or just a handful of reviews(ten or less) for a book over a week old is like having an empty restaurant. Your prospective readers rely on both the number of reviews and the content of the reviews to give them the confidence to buy your book.

How many reviews are enough?

According to Scribe Media:

"How Many Reviews Do I Need? For a minimum, you should try to get 20 reviews within the first two months after your book release date. That shows your book has traction with real readers. At around fifty reviews, you are probably good to go."[12]

According to CS Lakin:

"The magic number to start the ball rolling in this free promotion is 50. Fifty reviews merit cross-promotion and ranking your book higher than others in the same categories based on search terms. With 75 reviews, Amazon is triggered to send email blasts to customers who've bought similar books. Amazon utilizes customer data to provide relevant recommendations."[13]

Book review content is essential. I am not talking about all five-star reviews. That is not realistic or natural. If you have only a handful of reviews and they are all five-star, it is okay. To have twenty-five or more five-star reviews looks suspect. No one—not even N.Y. Times or WSJ bestsellers—gets all five-star reviews. As an example [see image below], Atomic Habits by James Clear, which has spent over 200 weeks on the N.Y. Times Bestseller List and over 287 weeks on Amazon as one of the top twenty books in their entire store, has an average rating of 4.8 out of 5 stars across 133, 562 reviews. Even Atomic Habits, a top bestselling book, gets one-star reviews, though not many of them.

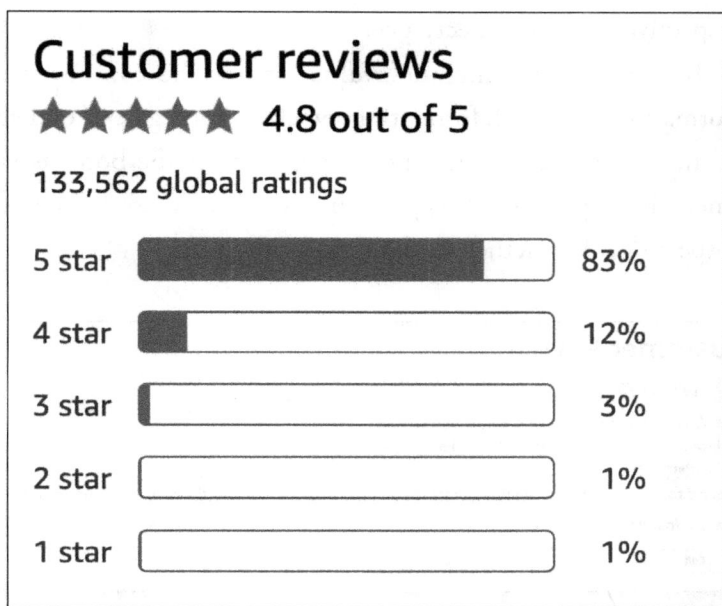

Customer reviews

★★★★★ 4.8 out of 5

133,562 global ratings

5 star		83%
4 star		12%
3 star		3%
2 star		1%
1 star		1%

Example customer reviews – Atomic Habits

While we can't know the identity of most book reviewers, we assume they are unbiased people who have read the book. While we don't know them personally, we trust their reviews, just like a restaurant review from a stranger on Yelp.

The content of book reviews is a great supplement to the book description, A+ content, and all information provided by the author or publisher.

Reviewers share their experiences with the book, which can help address prospective readers' questions and potential buying objections. These are often things that the author may not have thought to mention in their description or A+ Content.

They also include critical feedback on the book from the perspective of the prospect's peers.

The reviews can include evaluations of the content itself, information presented, formatting, typeface, pacing, level of detail, and more. They can reflect positive aspects of the book as well as negative aspects or disappointments. All of these help a cold prospect decide whether the book is for them.

Customer Review

👤 LeftBank ✓

★★☆☆☆ **Hard to get past the poor formatting**
Reviewed in the United States on December 4, 2020
Verified Purchase
I started to read the book, as the title caught my attention. Hard to get past the poor formatting to read it.
2 people found this helpful

(Edit) (Delete) | Permalink

Example negative customer review

As you can see from the customer review above, the twostar review which highlights the poor formatting of the book was found to be helpful by two people. That means that at least two people probably passed on buying this book because of this review. Using the accepted 'book review math' for the ratio of buyers to reviews (one out of thirty) could mean that as many as sixty prospective buyers might have passed on this book.

Or we know that not everyone who is browsing or buys a book leaves a review, so this number is probably a lot higher, though we have no way of knowing.

A quick scan of the book listing will tell the prospect how many reviews a book has, and that number alone may be enough to cause them to decide to click onto the next book, or to continue checking out the book by reading some of the reviews.

Amazon allows you to search for books within a category based on the number and quality of the reviews. If you want to search for leadership books with over twenty-five reviews or all leadership books with over four-star reviews, you can. Amazon enabled this search by book review quality and quantity because they know how much reviews matter and impact buying decisions.

"Social proof is a psychological phenomenon where people assume the actions of others in an attempt to reflect correct behavior for a given situation. In essence, it's the notion that, since others are doing it, I should be doing it, too."[14]

Social proof is the phenomenon whereby people validate decision-making by observing the behavior of others. It is the reason we ask for other's opinions, assume restaurants with waiting lists must be great, and the driver behind showcasing product reviews and customer testimonials. In the online marketing space, this translates to more people reading your content, social commenting or sharing, and buying a book based on the number of reviews.

Back to the restaurant analogy, people will ask friends about their dining experience or seek out online reviews on platforms such as Yelp before making a reservation and dining at a restaurant.

They look for the same type of feedback from book reviews.

Book reviewers can be peers of your prospective book buyers. As such, reviews can offer a fresh perspective on the book, as well as evaluate it in what is likely a similar way that the prospect would. Peer reviewers can offer:

- Honest feedback on their experience with the book
- Observations about how it was helpful to them or why it didn't fulfill their wishes or expectations
- Specific aspects of the book that they liked

When a reviewer shares specific positives about how the book helped them, it can help sway prospects who are looking for a book to solve a similar problem to buy.

Negatives or other specific feedback in a review can help the prospect manage their expectations of what they will glean from the book. It can also help answer questions they had in their mind that they were seeking answers to before deciding if they want to buy the book.

The specifics found in reviews can benefit the author in improving the book listing. They can use this feedback to improve their book description or A+ Content so buyer questions are answered upfront and prospective readers are kept from wondering. This can lead to converting more prospects to buyers. This feedback review can also inform authors of potential additions or edits to the book if they plan to do a revised version in the future.

There is gold in book reviews for authors. While most authors tell me they dread getting a one-star review, it can provide some of the most valuable information you receive. That is if you try and use it to improve your book or your book listing.

Remember, a one or two-star review, or a particularly harsh or negative one, could also be a troll and have nothing to do with your book. Because reviewers can be anonymous and hide behind a handle rather than use their real name, it creates an easy opportunity for someone having a bad day to take it out in your book review. They will only take the review down if it violates Amazon's terms of service. It will be up to you to read the review and decide if it is legitimate and useful.

Organic, Free, Professional, and Paid Book Review Campaigns

Types of Reviews

There are three types of book reviews: customer, professional, and editorial. This chapter is focused primarily on customer reviews.

Let's define each of these reviews and where they appear on your book listing page.

Customer reviews. Anyone who has bought over fifty dollars' worth of products on Amazon can leave a review. They don't have to have purchased the book to leave a review, though reviews left by someone who has bought the book are marked as 'verified' and, for apparent reasons, carry more weight.

An unverified review could be from someone who read the book but didn't purchase it on Amazon.

These appear under the starred Customer Reviews section on a book listing page.

Professional reviews. These are subjective book reviews performed by book editors or publishing professionals. They include a summary, critique of the book's execution, opinion, and insights. They may also include a recommendation to read the book. Many are paid reviews*, contracted via a service provider such as Kirkus Reviews or Indie Reader.

*While it is against Amazon's terms of service to pay for customer reviews, it is allowable to pay for professional book reviews.

While these reviews don't have their own section on Amazon, they are often included in the Editorial Reviews section, quoted in the book description, or even highlighted on a book cover.

Editorial Reviews. These are unpaid, critical assessments of a book by industry experts and reviewers in the media. They objectively note the strengths and weaknesses based on professional standards, helping potential readers understand if the book aligns with their preferences.

These appear under the Editorial Reviews section on a book listing page. They may also be quoted in the book description or on the top of the front or back cover. Editorial Reviews are covered more extensively later in Chapter 9.

It is worth noting that customers leaving book reviews on Amazon can post using a handle or username – their real identity is not shown. With editorial reviews, the true identity of the commenter is shown along with the title. In the case of professional reviews, for the most part, the outlet giving the review is named, but not the actual reviewer.

How to get book reviews

Getting book reviews is one of the most important jobs of authors, no matter their genre. I recommend thinking of it as an ongoing process or initiative and not just something to do during the first month after your book is published.

There are several ways to encourage readers to leave book reviews. Here are some methods that have been effective for authors.

Ask. This is the simplest yet often overlooked method for garnering book reviews that authors can take. Readers need to be asked, encouraged and reminded to leave reviews.

One way to promote your book while reminding people to leave a review is to screenshot a glowing review from Amazon and share it with your network and on social media. You can be direct and say something such as, "I'm Humbled by this great review of my book. If you enjoyed it, please leave a review. I'd appreciate it!" Provide the link to leave a review for ease of use.

While Amazon doesn't provide a way to contact its customers, you can leave a message inside your book. At Simply Good Press, we do this at the end of some of our books, asking the purchaser to leave a review.

Review Trades. You can trade reviews with fellow authors. Trades can be done one-on-one with authors you know or by signing up with a service like Pubby.com that connects you with people willing to trade reviews. You can also buy credits, which work as a form of currency on Pubby, to be used instead of having to read and review other authors' works in exchange for getting your book reviewed.

Paid review services. While you can't pay a reader to review your book under Amazon's terms of service, you can hire a service that will connect you with readers who enjoy getting free books in exchange for writing customer reviews. Some packages include verified reviews.

Get the word out about your book.

The Media.

While reaching out to the media is a less direct way to encourage book reviews, it helps raise awareness and get in front of many more potential readers. It also acts as an endorsement for your book. The media only interviews some people, only people they select. Their audience looks to them for recommendations, which they trust more than they would if they had a cold encounter with your book on the internet.

To leverage the media for your book, pursue interviews on radio, TV, podcasts, blogs, or print publications.

We know that one to ten percent of readers leave a review, so you can expect up to ten reviews for one hundred readers. Getting in front of more prospective readers increases your chances of more sales.

Book Reader Newsletters. These are promotional newsletters that have huge reader followings, segregated by genre. Some newsletters are free, and others require a fee to list your book. They also require you to offer your book for free or at a discount to their list. The benefit of this is that in addition to getting in front of many prospective readers instantly, the limited time offer (free or discount)motivates the list to act immediately or lose the opportunity. While these newsletters don't give you the email addresses of the readers, you can expect a boost in reviews after a promotion. If you have a review request in your book, that will also help encourage more reviews.

Goodreads Giveaway. This is a great way to generate buzz and new readers like newsletters. It has a high chance of generating reviews for your book, as Goodreads is a community of book lovers that helps readers find and share books they love. The majority of interactions on their site are based on commenting and reviewing books.

An additional benefit of a Goodreads giveaway is the visibility it can give your book. That is because all interested readers must opt-in for the promotion. By doing so, the giveaway prize book gets automatically added to their 'want-to-read' shelf on Goodreads, which is publicly visible to their entire network. This is like having lots of people talking about your book at the same time.

Collect email addresses. An important way to garner more book reviews is by actively building an email list. With it, you can nurture your reader relationships and ask them to leave a review for your book. As mentioned, Amazon doesn't share emails with you. However, there are ways to get readers to join your email list or follow you on social media. One of the best ways to motivate readers to opt into your list is to offer them an irresistible bonus.

We offer downloadable or online bonus content that they get only when they opt-in with their email address. We create a page in the book to inform readers about the bonuses and where to collect them. Some authors mention bonus content on their book covers. See our bonus content at the end of this book as an example.

Bonus content can be made up of anything related to the book that adds value or further enhances the reader experience. This content can be worksheets, checklists, a sample chapter, audio, or video.

The bonus content offered in the back of this book illustrates how to set it up.

CHAPTER NINE

Additional Tools

A Book Series

A book series is subtle yet powerful for optimization.

It gives you additional real estate on your book listing, showcasing the series title, which is also a hyperlink under your author's name. It links to your series page, which provides additional, searchable, real estate for you on Amazon displaying all related books. The series title is searchable, and therefore can be keyword optimized to help you be discovered more by your ideal readers. This gives you an additional way to add SEO value to your book listings. Your keyword selection can include individual words or a few word phrases.

Prospective readers will view you favorably as a multi-book author, adding to your credibility. Additionally, it can increase sales significantly as people who found you during their topic search will likely be interested in the other books in the series. If they enjoyed one of the books in your series, they already know, like, and trust you. They are warm leads at that point, so you don't need to sell them on you.

Video

Author videos and review videos are the two types of videos that can be added to your book listing.

The power of video is very compelling. As humans, we relate to seeing another human and can create a deeper connection than text alone. Video adds trust and credibility. We can see a real person behind the video, such as the author or reviewer.

It also provides edutainment. Videos have become more popular, and some people enjoy consuming them more than reading content. They appeal on a few levels and can be faster for viewers to process, as the brain processes visuals faster than text.

An author video can introduce the author to prospective readers, humanizing them and building more know, like, and trust. It is also an opportunity to provide added value and additional information to the readers, giving them a peek behind the scenes. You can also share what inspired you to write the book.

A greeting from the author can provide a warm and human touch—a face behind the book. From a real estate optimization point of view, videos expand your listing with a video thumbnail added to it. These images can draw the eye and create intrigue.

Review Videos

While you can't compel a reviewer to leave a video, some will do so alone. You can invite reviewers you know to create and upload a video review for your book. Video reviews add credibility, as we can see real people speaking and feel their authenticity. They also keep people on your book page longer, deepening their connection and interest and increasing sales.

Editorial Reviews

Traditionally, Editorial Reviews evaluate a piece of work by an expert, such as a publisher, editor, or the media. They are usually critical analyses that enhance the work and enlighten the audience. They don't offer an opinion about whether the book is good or bad.

Editorial reviews on Amazon are typically short, with one to two sentences of positive statements or blurbs. While these have no known effect on Amazon SEO, they provide powerful third-party credibility, building trust and buyer confidence.

Trust is such an important factor in consumer buying decisions that extensive market surveys are devoted to consumer trust, such as those conducted by research firms near Thales or Nielsen. The public has come to mistrust marketers and brands, which extends to unknown authors on Amazon. Even with a credible and professional-looking book listing, prospective readers seek confirmation that the book is good. They look at the Amazon starred book review section, and they look to the editorial reviews to help them learn more about the product and inform their decision whether to buy the book. According to Amazon: "Editorial reviews are different from customer reviews, as they are transcribed directly from reputable sources."[15]

People look to this section to learn what professionals say about the book. One key difference between editorial reviews and other book reviews is that editorial reviews can't be anonymous—they require the source to be named and displayed alongside them.

- Shoppers take notice of the editorial review section if it exists, and it is easily readable and attention-grabbing.
- Most don't read the editorial review itself but instead pay more attention to who said it and what qualifies them to speak about this book (something I call the "qualifier").
- The sweet spot is six to ten editorial reviews. If you have fewer, shoppers tend to skip it; if you have more, they generally disregard it.

The Editorial Reviews section is a feature of a detail page and is intended to provide customers with descriptive information about a title. This is not to say that starred customer reviews are not valid or valuable. Still, it is important to keep them in perspective and contrast them with editorial reviews, which always showcase the reviewer's name and title.

Jane Friedman: "Amazon editorial reviews are one of the most underrated tools in a self-publishing author's arsenal—that's because most authors either don't know what they are or how to access them. Editorial reviews are book evaluations usually written by an editor or expert in the book's genre or field. You can find them on your book's sales page, just above the About the Author section."[16]

Gathering Editorial Reviews

As I mentioned, your editorial review doesn't have to come from a recognized celebrity. What does matter is the person's credentials or title. Here are a few examples of types of ideal profiles for editorial reviewers:

- The media (if your book gets reviewed in a media outlet, you can and should pull a quote to use)
- Professional Book Reviewers or Awards (Kirkus Reviews, International Book Awards)
- Recognized celebrities
- Best-selling authors
- People with professional titles such as M.D., Ph.D., Esq.
- People with titles such as head of x-association, president of x-company

Your book may garner some reviews somewhat organically, such as from the media. For the most part, though, if you want endorsements, you must conduct an outreach campaign and ask individuals to write them for your book. I detail this process on my blog in a series entitled Celebrity Endorsements - How to get them for your book[17] and in my Celebrity Book Endorsement training guide.[18]

Formatting Editorial Reviews: Best Practices & Maximizing Results

As a PR professional, I was confident that the most important part of the editorial review is the title of the person leaving the review more than any other aspect. This fact was confirmed in a study by Dave Chesson of Kindlepreneur https://bit.ly/selfpubbook2.[19] He could chart and analyze where viewer attention focuses on a book listing using heat map technology, which tracks website visitor activity, particularly where the eyes focus on a page.

"... we conducted a test and found that not only do shoppers pay attention to editorial reviews, but these reviews influenced shoppers to buy at a noticeable rate...when done correctly." - Dave Chesson[20]

To showcase the reviewer's credentials, here is the best way to set up an editorial review:

Quote | **Name, Title**

"A comprehensive book that every entrepreneur should read." - **John Smith, CEO of XMark Company, 3x Inc. 500 List**

As a reviewer, John Smith would be considered highly qualified as his CEO credential is one of the highest levels an entrepreneur or professional can achieve in business, and he is assumedly highly familiar with the subject matter. The 3x Inc. 500 List mention is an additional qualifier as it is a list of the fastest-growing privately held companies in the United States. It is a prestigious list of the nation's most successful private companies and has become the hallmark of entrepreneurial success and the place where future household names first make their mark.

Editorial Reviews

Review

"Brave, compelling and thoroughly original! Author Wendy Ryan challenges our traditional notions of leadership like no one else. Read Learn Lead Lift and take your own leadership skills to the next level!"-- **Marshall Goldsmith, Thinkers 50 #1 Executive Coach and only two-time #1 Leadership Thinker in the world.**

"Learn Lead Lift is a must-read for everyone--even people who don't consider themselves traditional leaders. In this hands-on guide, author Wendy Ryan captures the mindsets, skill sets and behaviors that anyone can adopt to become a better leader." -- **Beverly Kaye, Co-Author of Love 'Em or Lose 'Em, Help Them Grow or Watch Them Go and Up is Not the Only Way**

"Self-awareness is indispensable in leaders, but as Wendy Ryan notes, it's insufficient. To be effective, leaders must also be able to adjust their thinking and behavior in response to their awareness. Learn Lead Lift is filled with these kinds of valuable insights that challenge leadership orthodoxy. I found valuable lessons in every chapter." -- **Sally Helgesen, Author of How Women Rise, The Female Advantage, The Web of Inclusion**

"In Learn Lead Lift, Wendy Ryan offers an unflinching look at what's required to be an effective leader today. Filled with stories, examples, actionable strategies and challenges, this book is essential reading for anyone aspiring to (or already in) leadership." -- **Julie Winkle Giulioni, Co-Author of Help Them Grow or Watch Them Go: Career Conversations Organizations Need and Employees Want**

Editorial Reviews example using HTML formatting

As you can see from our example, it utilizes bold and non-bolded text. These are features offered by Amazon's proprietary HTML, which is available for your editorial review. By highlighting the Name and Title, you are calling it out to make it easier to find by the prospect and subliminally letting them know that this is the more important information.

Even if John Smith is not known to the prospective book buyer, his credentials are impressive and trustworthy and can help nudge a prospect past uncertainty into buying your book. These reviews carry weight based on a person's title, not their celebrity or recognition factor. They don't need to be known or recognized by the prospect to influence them and gain trust.

Note: Editorial reviews appear on your Amazon book listing, but unlike all the other author tools mentioned in this book, they are not added via the KDP platform. Editorial reviews can be added to your book via your Amazon Author Central account, as discussed earlier in this book.

Great on Kindle

A little-known feature available to authors, if you qualify, is called Great on Kindle. Amazon has a distinction for books that meet a high level, which is the exacting standard for eBooks. It is currently only available for select nonfiction titles

Amazon describes it as follows: "Great on Kindle is an Amazon program to help customers discover high-quality nonfiction eBooks. Great on Kindle eBooks offer enhanced features that readers value." Think of this as Amazon's Good Housekeeping Seal top quality award.

Great on Kindle is valuable to authors and book optimization for two main reasons:

1. Enhanced Credibility
   - Adds additional credibility to your book, showcasing to readers that it has passed the rigorous Amazon quality standards for an eBook.
   - Removes buyer doubt that the book is well-formatted and professionally created.
   - Enhances your book listing with a prominent banner displayed to let browsers know that you have earned this distinction

2. Additional Searchability and Discoverability
   This designation places places your book in an additional category, Great on Kindle. This is a new, small searchable category for readers who are seeking well-formatted nonfiction books.

CONCLUSION

Amazon offers you many tools to help you get discovered by your ideal readers and sell more books.

You can think of them as tools for decorating your online bookstore and enhancing staffing with knowledgeable salespeople. The more information you provide in your book listing, the better your chance of converting new Amazon traffic to buyers.

Earlier, I mentioned cold traffic and the importance of building trust with prospects. A professional listing helps you do this. Social proof in the form of book reviews, blurbs, media reviews, and any other third-party recognition and recommendations adds more trust. It's not just the author saying their book is great, which is less trustworthy and even suspect.

You should strive for a well-optimized profile with as much social proof as possible. More editorial and positive reviews make your book more credible and reduce buying hesitation.

Finally, remember that optimizing your book is an ongoing process, and listings should be updated regularly. Did you get a new book endorsement or review from the media? Add it to the editorial reviews section promptly so that it can start working for you on Amazon.

REFERENCES

1. Dimitrije Curcic, Amazon Publishing Statistics, Wordsrated, January 12, 2023 https://wordsrated.com/amazon-publishing-statistics/
2. Curcic, Amazon Publishing Statics
3. A+ Content: Increase Sales with Engaging Product Listings, https://sell.amazon.com/tools/a-content
4. Most Visited Websites in the United States, SEMRUSH, Updated July 2024, https://www.semrush.com/website/top/united-states/all/
5. Curcic, Amazon Publishing Statistics
6. Dave Chesson, The Art and Science to Amazon Editorial Reviews, Kindlepreneur, December 13th, 2022 https://kindlepreneur.com/amazon-editorial-reviews/
7. Facts About Book Metadata and Why It's Critical to Your Publishing Success, IngramSpark, December 27, 2018 https://www.ingramspark.com/blog/7-facts-about-book-metadata
8. Author Central, Kindle Direct Publishing https://kdp.amazon.com/en_US/help/topic/G200644310
9. A+ Content: Increase Sales with Engaging Product Listings
10. Imagery Vs. Text: Which does the brain prefer, World of Learning, https://www.learnevents.com/learning-insights/imagery-vs-text-which-does-the-brain-prefer/

11. Endless Referrals, Bob Burg, https://endlessreferrals.com/

12. Tucker Max, How To Get Reviews For Your Book On Amazon, Scribe Media, https://scribemedia.com/amazon-book-reviews/

13. CS Lakin, The Best Way to Rack Up Book Reviews on Amazon, Live Write Thrive, February 21, 2022 https://www.livewritethrive.com/2022/02/21/the-best-way-to-rack-up-book-reviews-on-amazon/

14. What is Social Proof, Glossary, Dynamic Yield https://www.dynamicyield.com/es/glossary/social-proof/

15. Editorial Reviews, Amazon Author Central, https://author.amazon.com/help/GFUAUZE7BYCD7H4D

16. Jane Friedman, Amazon Editorial Reviews: Are You Using This Incredible Section?, JaneFriedman.com, Jul 13, 2020, https://janefriedman.com/amazon-editorial-reviews-are-you-using-this-incredible-section/

17. Jane Tabachnick, Celebrity Endorsements - How to get them for your book, JaneTabachnick.com, https://www.janetabachnick.com/how-to-get-celebrity-endorsements/

18. Jane Tabachnick, Celebrity Book Endorsement Guide ?? Title?? Link to buy

19. Dave Chesson, The Art and Science to Amazon Editorial Reviews, Kindlepreneur, December 13th, 2022, https://kindlepreneur.com/amazon-editorial-reviews/

20. Dave Chesson, The Art and Science to Amazon Editorial Reviews

GLOSSARY

Algorithm
An algorithm is a process or set of rules to be followed in calculations or other problem-solving operations, especially by a computer. Search algorithms work to retrieve information stored within a database such as Amazon's book catalog.

A Plus Content
Amazon A+ Content is a feature that enables sellers to personalize their product detail pages with engaging text, images, videos, and more. It helps authors showcase their books by highlighting features and benefits and providing additional information to help prospects make buying decisions.

Author Page / Author Profile
Your Author Page is your unique book landing page on Amazon via Author Central. It can include your bio, headshot, and a listing of all your books on one page.

Author Central
Amazon Author Central lets you create your Author Page to share the most up-to-date information about yourself and your books with millions of readers. It helps readers find books easily and in one place.

Book Layout Design

A book layout design refers to how the text, photos, tables, and other elements are arranged within the pages of a book. The role of a book layout designer is to pick out the right typographic elements and arrange them to make the book's content readable and aesthetically appealing to readers.

Book Listing Page

A book listing page is the page on Amazon where a book is listed; customers can find information about it and buy it. It is also called a product detail page.

Book Description

Content on your book's Amazon listing page is often a reader's first experience with your book. A well-written book description is essential for enticing readers. It summarizes a book's content to give readers a glimpse into what it is about and is often the first impression of your story's content and writing style.

Book Reviews

A book review is a detailed and evaluative analysis of a book. It includes a summary of the content, an assessment of the book's value, and a recommendation for potential readers.

Customer Reviews

Amazon customer reviews are public ratings and written feedback from customers about products they've purchased on Amazon. Reviews can include a star rating on a scale of one to five, a written explanation, and photos or videos.

Professional book reviews

Professional book reviews are written by experts who work for reliable organizations such as newspapers, magazines, and online platforms. They aim to offer knowledgeable and well-informed opinions on magazines, books, and newspapers. There are service providers that you can pay to have them provide a professional review of your book (these are acceptable to Amazon, though paying individuals for reviews is not).

Best Seller Rank (BSR)

The Amazon Best Sellers Rank (BSR) is a metric that indicates how well a product is selling compared to other items within the same category on Amazon. It is represented by a number, with a lower BSR indicating that a product is selling better.

Categories

The categories in the Amazon Store act as sections where customers can locate your book. These categories, such as history and cooking, are similar to the sections in a physical bookstore.

Cover design

Cover design is the primary tool for piquing a reader's interest or making a book or magazine stand out. It must look visually appealing while highlighting the details readers need to know about the book.

Editorial Reviews

Traditionally, an evaluation of a piece of work by a professional expert such as a publisher, editor, or the media, editorial reviews are usually in the form of a critical analysis aimed at enhancing the work and enlightening the audience as to whether the book is a good fit for them. It is also an optional section on the Amazon Book Listings page that is often populated by short one to two-sentence positive statements or blurbs about a book written by a celebrity, the media, or a credentialed expert.

Great on Kindle

Great on Kindle is an Amazon program that helps customers discover high-quality nonfiction eBooks. It offers enhanced features that readers value. This program is currently for select nonfiction titles and in select Amazon Marketplaces.

Hypertext Markup Language (HTML) for Amazon

Hypertext Markup Language [HTML] is a markup language for structuring web page content and telling web browsers how to display text, images, and media. Amazon book descriptions and editorial reviews can be formatted using Amazon HTML, an abbreviated version of HTML with more limited options.

Indexing

Being indexed on Amazon means that your product will appear in the search results when someone searches for a keyword related to your product. For example, if you're indexed for "leadership book," your product will appear when someone searches for "leadership book" on Amazon.

Kindle Direct Publishing (KDP)

Kindle Direct Publishing is a self-publishing e-book platform launched by Amazon.com. It lets authors and publishers publish their books to the Amazon Book Store.

Keywords

Keywords are specific terms and phrases that denote what a book or article is about. Authors and publishers must choose the appropriate keywords so that their books appear when readers search for a specific topic.

Kindle

Kindle refers to a book format and a reading device created by Amazon. A Kindle book is an electronic book (e-book) designed to be read on a Kindle e-reader or other device with the Kindle app installed. These books are published and distributed by Amazon and can be purchased and downloaded through Amazon's website or the Kindle app.

Metadata

Book metadata contains information that can help a book reach its target audience. It should tell the reader the title of the book, who the author and publisher are, when it was published, what its genre is, and its ISBN so that readers can find your book. The metadata should also include a short description to give readers a glimpse of the book's content.

Optimization

Book optimization is the process of enhancing a book listing to make it more easily discovered and more appealing to visitors by utilizing all available Amazon features.

Print on Demand

Print on demand (POD) refers to the process of printing and binding books only when someone places an order for them. This process significantly reduces the risks and costs often present with bulk-printing large quantities of books that are not guaranteed to sell.

Publisher

A publisher creates and handles the distribution of books and other materials. They are often associated with books and magazines but may also be associated with music production and journals.

RESOURCES LIST

Keyword and Category Research Tools
- Publisher Rocket https://simplygood--rocket.thrivecart.com/publisher-rocket/
- Kindle Spy KD Spy https://simplygood--leadsclick.thrivecart.com/kdspy-v5/

Book Reviews
- Pubby https://pubby.co/

Book Promotion Newsletters
- The Fussy Librarian https://www.thefussylibrarian.com/
- Best Promo Sites -2024 List https://davidgaughran.com/best-promo-sites-books/
- Goodreads Giveaway https://www.goodreads.com/giveaway

Professional Book Reviews (Paid)
- Kirkus Reviews https://www.kirkusreviews.com/indie-reviews/
- Indie Reader https://indiereader.com/get-a-book-review/

Editorial Reviews
- Celebrity Book Endorsement Guide – training guide https://jmtonline.systeme.io/92f8f88f

Amazon Feature Guidelines:

- A+ Content Guidelines https://kdp.amazon.com/en_US/ help/topic/G4WB7VPPEAREHAAD
- Editorial Review Guidelines: https://author.amazon.com/ help/GFUAUZE7BYCD7H4D
- Author Central Guidelines: https://kdp.amazon.com/en_US/ help/topic/G200644310

Accessing Amazon Features:

- Main Amazon author dashboard: https://kdp.amazon.com/
- A+ Content and Author Central– in KDP dashboard under the marketing tab
- Author Central – can also be created via its own site at https://author.amazon.com/

GIFT

Free Gift

I've put together some valuable resources to help you optimize your book listing.

Download your copy here: https://bit.ly/selfpublishingbonus

ABOUT THE AUTHOR

Jane Tabachnick is an award-winning book publishing consultant and bestselling author. She is celebrated for her expertise in transforming experts into influential, published authors amplifying their visibility, impact, and profitability.

As the founder of Simply Good Press, a premier book publishing and promotion agency, Jane leads a dedicated team that guides clients from idea to acclaimed author status. Her mentorship has helped over 250 authors achieve bestseller status and secure significant media coverage in prestigious outlets, cementing their positions as industry authorities.

Named one of Fast Company's top 100 people online, Jane's thought leadership and insights have been featured across respected media outlets, including *Inc.*, *Crain's NY*, *The NY Enterprise Report*, *The Star-Ledger*, *Environmental Leader*, *CNN*, *Houston Magazine*, *Spa Magazine*, *Women's Wear Daily*, and leading podcasts.

Jane has also contributed to the entrepreneurial landscape through educational initiatives, creating training programs for the Fashion Institute of Technology and the American Women's Economic Development Corporation. Additionally, she has developed impactful courses and resources designed specifically to help authors enhance their influence and reach.

For more information on mentorship, courses, and exclusive writing retreats, visit www.janetabachnick.com

To inquire about speaking engagements or podcast appearances, please contact us at www.janetabachnick.com/contact

www.ingramcontent.com/pod-product-compliance
Lightning Source LLC
Chambersburg PA
CBHW070026030426
42335CB00017B/2311